Bad Cats

Bad Cats

A Collection of Feline Pranks and Practical Jokes

Rick Stromoski

CONTEMPORARY
BOOKS
A TRIBUNE NEW MEDIA COMPANY

Library of Congress Cataloging-in-Publication Data

Stromoski, Rick.
    Bad cats / Rick Stromoski.
       p.   cm.
    ISBN 0-8092-3478-5 (paper)
    1. Cats—Caricatures and cartoons.   2. Pictorial wit and humor,
American.   I. Title.
    NC1429.S74A4   1995
    741.5'973—dc20   94-42754
                                                  CIP

Published by Contemporary Books, Inc.
Two Prudential Plaza, Chicago, Illinois 60601-6790
Manufactured in the United States of America
International Standard Book Number: 0-8092-3478-5
10   9   8   7   6   5   4   3   2   1

For Crusty

8

14

17

35

42

70

80

104

About the Artist

Rick Stromoski is a full-time cartoonist and humorous illustrator whose work has appeared in such publications as *Playboy*, *Saturday Evening Post*, *Esquire*, *Harper's*, and *Good Housekeeping*.

He has illustrated bestselling greeting cards for companies such as Recycled Paper Greetings and Renaissance Greetings and has been nominated for the prestigious Louie Award for outstanding design in the greeting card industry nine times, winning on four occasions.

Rick's work has also appeared in the CBS television movie *Who Gets the Friends?*, starring Jill Clayburgh as a divorced cartoonist. His syndicated newspaper strip, "A Dog and His Boy," ran nationally in 1988.

Originally from Edison, New Jersey, he traveled west and lived for ten years in the Los Angeles area. Rick and his wife, Danna, and their baby girl, Molly, along with their dog, Odin, and cat, Crusty, now live in the historic district of Suffield, Connecticut.